THE
ABC BOOK
OF
MANNERS
FOR
CHILDREN

by
Shelby Hill
with
Jerri Beth Heffington

Illustrations by
Helmut Barnett

State House Press
Austin, Texas
1988

Library of Congress Cataloging-in-Publication Data

Hill, Shelby, 1953—
The ABC book of manners for children /
by Shelby Hill, Jerri Beth Heffington;
illustrations by Helmut Barnett.
p. cm.
Summary: An introduction, in rhymed text and
illustrations, to the letters of the alphabet
and basic rules of good behavior.
ISBN 0-938349-32-5 : $16.95
1. Children—Conduct of life. 2. Etiquette for children
and teenagers. [1. Alphabet. 2. Etiquette.]
I. Heffington, Jerri Beth, 1941- . II. Barnett, Helmut,
1946- ill. III. Title.

BJ1631.H49 1988   88-24082
395'.122—dc19   CIP
[E]   AC

State House Press
P.O. Box 15247 • Austin, Texas 78761

Printed in the United States of America

Dedicated with love to:

Jerry and Frank Hill
Hannelore and Gerald Barnett
Anna Beth Percival and Ann Walker Heffington

A
is for
answers.

There may be times
you'll wonder

What you should
say or do.

We hope to give
some **answers**

In this book written
just for you!

B

**is for
bath.**

To take a **bath**
  is lots of fun

But some things
  you should know:

Use little water,
  clean the tub

And put toys back
  where they go.

C

is for car.

When mom or dad
   is driving

There's lots to
   think about.

So in the **car**
   put seatbelts on

And please, oh please,
   don't shout!

D
is for
door.

A **door** is for going
   in or out,

But has anyone
   told you this?

If you open doors
   for those who can't

You just might
   get a kiss.

E

is for eating.

When **eating** in
  a restaurant

Or at your
  kitchen table

Sit up straight,
  put your feet on the floor

(As well as you
  are able!)

F

is for
finger foods.

At mealtime it's easy
to use your hands,

Such little effort
it takes.

But only **finger foods**
are for fingers,

Like cookies, candies,
and cupcakes.

G

is for greeting.

Do you know
what words to use

When **greeting**
someone new?

"It's so very nice
to meet you" or

"Hello, how do
you do?"

RIU

MORE
FISH →

H

is for
hands.

Who knows why
  it is so much fun

To touch something
  or someone else.

Unless you are asked
  to use your **hands**

Please keep them
  to yourself.

I

is for interrupt.

If you see a
  person talking

And there's something
  you must do

Never **interrupt,**
  instead use a sign

To say, "I need to
  talk with you."

J

is for
jumping.

I can think of
  many reasons

For not **jumping**
  on a bed.

The best, of course,
  is that you might

Land right upon
  your head.

K

is for
kindness.

Kindness is a
  perfect word

Its meaning holds
  so much.

A word of caring
  to one who's sad

And a heart you will
  tenderly touch.

L

**is for
leaving.**

When the time has
come for **leaving**

It's easy to just
walk away,

But friends will want you
to come again soon

If you say, "Thanks,
I had a great day!"

M
is for mistake.

If you do something
  by **mistake**

An apology
  is polite.

So simply say,
  "Forgive me, please."

Then try to
  make things right.

N
is for
napkin.

Whether it is
  big or small

Or white or blue
  or green,

A **napkin** goes
  upon your lap

Not where it
  can be seen.

O

is for
overnight.

One day you will
  be old enough

To be an **overnight**
  guest.

Take all your
  manners with you

And let everyone
  get some rest!

P

is for
please.

It's one of the first words
that you learned

So it should come
with ease.

When asking a favor
of anyone

Begin or end your
sentence with **"please"**.

Q

is for
quiet.

It's okay to have fun
and play

In your neighborhood
park or pool.

But **quiet** is the word
to remember

In your library,
church or school.

R

is for respect.

People or things that are older than you:

Your grandma, a painting, a tree,

Deserve **respect,** so take care to treat them

Kindly and courteously.

S

is for sharing.

Sharing something
that you like

May not be fun,
it's true,

So try to remember
a happy time

When someone shared
with you.

T

is for
thank you.

For a gift, a visit
or any kind deed,

There's something you
always should do.

In person, by letter
or telephone call

Remember to say a
"Thank you!"

U

is for
utensil.

One knife, two forks,
   three spoons or more!

Which **utensil**
   should you use?

Just start from the
   outside and go in

Or watch a grownup
   to see which to choose.

V

is for valentine.

In February,
  on the 14th day

Hearts pass from
  hand to hand.

For those you love
  or care about

Make a **valentine,**
  small or grand.

W

is for waking.

When **waking** on
  Saturday morning

And it's time for
  your favorite cartoon,

Watch quietly, try to
  make not a sound,

Others may want to
  sleep until noon.

X

is for
eXample.

Children who are
younger than you

Can't help but do
as they see.

So though it doesn't
begin with an X,

An **eXample** you
often will be.

Y

is for yes.

When someone asks
  a question

And your answer
  is **Y-E-S,**

Avoid the words "yeah,"
  "yup" and "yo"

They're sure to
  cause distress.

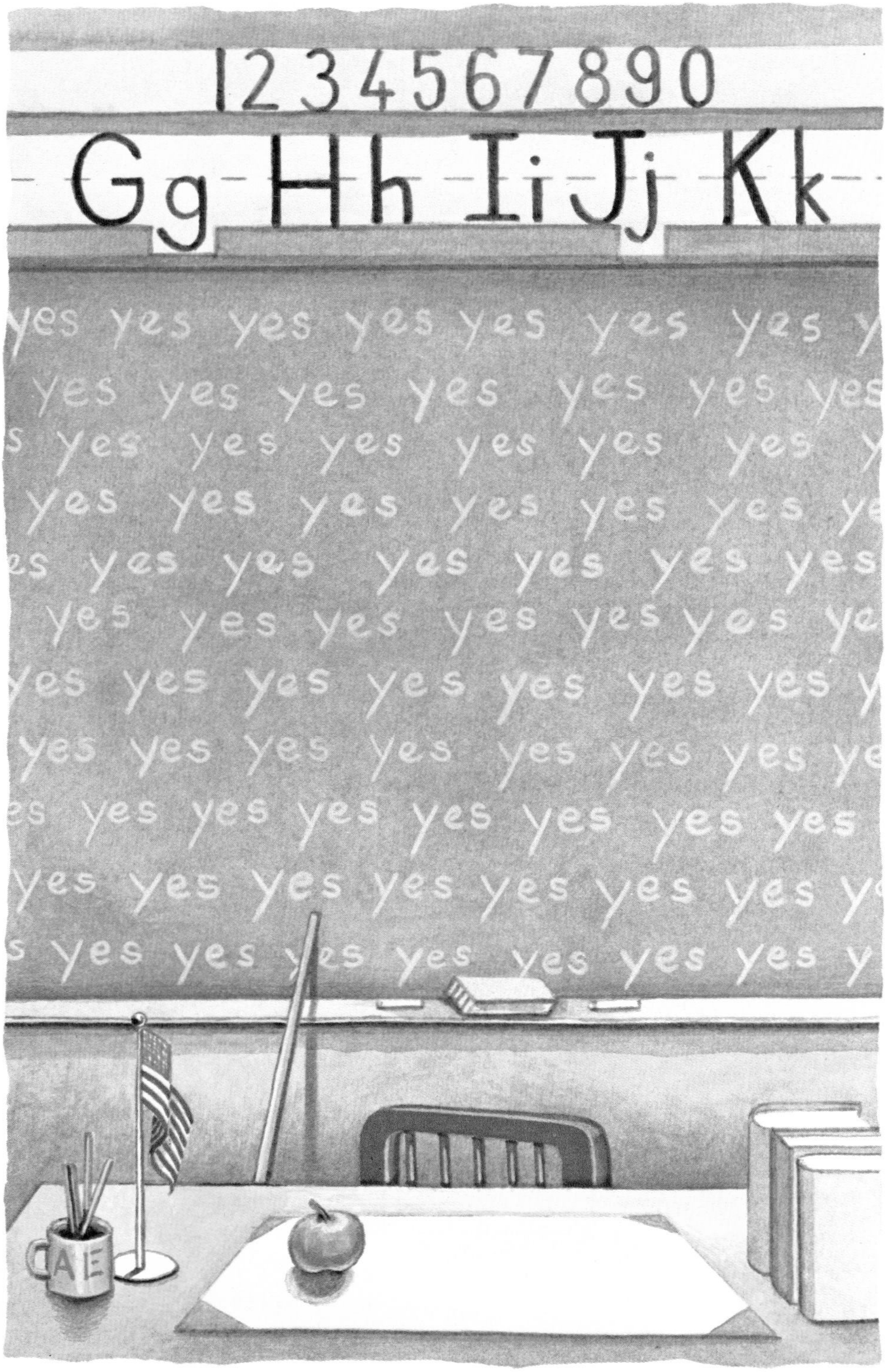
1234567890
Gg Hh Ii Jj Kk
yes yes yes yes yes yes yes
AE

Z

is for zoomed.

We **zoomed** along
through the ABC's.

Some rules may seem
quite new.

So if you forget,
here's a little hint:

"Treat others as you want
them to treat you."